FROM A CRIMINAL MIND TO THE MIND OF CHRIST

FROM A CRIMINAL MIND TO THE MIND OF CHRIST

Melody Wolfe

authorHOUSE®

AuthorHouse™
1663 Liberty Drive
Bloomington, IN 47403
www.authorhouse.com
Phone: 1 (800) 839-8640

Published by AuthorHouse 02/11/2015

ISBN: 978-1-4969-6972-9 (sc)
ISBN: 978-1-4969-6971-2 (e)

Print information available on the last page.

TABLE OF CONTENTS

DEDICATION

This book is dedicated to my Lord and Savior, Jesus Christ. You are the Author and Finisher of my faith. My heart is forever Yours!

ACKNOWLEDGEMENTS

Above all others, I would like to acknowledge Jehovah God. My Heavenly Father gave me the precious gift of His Son, Jesus, to wash and cleanse me from my sin. Father God has also given me His Spirit of Grace to live on the inside of me, who leads and directs my steps. My loving Heavenly Father has also given His written Word, the Bible, which has transformed my life and given me the inspiration to write this book.

Susan and Dana Hogg – As my parents, you have experienced both heartache and blessing from me. Your love, kindness and support during the most difficult times in my life have motivated me to pursue all that God has in store for me. I love you both with all my heart!

Hannah Wolfe – Since the day you were born, you have never ceased to be the reason I kept going when everything inside of me wanted to give up. It would be impossible for me to ask God for a lovelier daughter than what you are. Thank you for the gift of your love.

Lydia Wolfe – My precious baby! You fill the darkest days with rays of sunshine and happiness. You, as well as your sister, are treasures from God Himself. No mother could be prouder of their child than what I am of you.

Debbie Grandy – My heart is filled with gratitude for all your love and support. Thank you for allowing me the use of your resources for the purpose of writing this book. I appreciate all the times you gave me cups of coffee and an encouraging word as I wrote. You are more than an aunt – you are a very dear friend. I love you.

Pastor Ian MacFarlane – I cannot find words appropriate enough to convey just how much the Lord has used you in my life. I see all those in our church family who have been touched by your love and support. You use the gifts that God has given you for His glory, and I see the humility of Christ in you. Thank you for teaching me the important truth of depending on Christ.

Joy MacFarlane – I absolutely love our times together! You are a wonderful friend, as well as a Godly example of motherhood. You have the heart of a servant, and Christ is so beautiful in you and your family. Many servants go unnoticed or unrecognized, and I know that you do what you do from your heart, without seeking recognition. This is my opportunity to thank you for all the work you do "behind the scenes." God bless you.

Sgt. Kevin Murphy – Thank you for your hard work and dedication in serving and protecting our community. May the grace of God be lavished upon your life in abundance!

PRELUDE

Your adrenaline is high. You're running fast to get away, but they are catching up to you. You quickly discover there is no escape – they have you cornered. You are forced to comply, so you drop to the ground and they handcuff you. You know where you are headed.

You enter the doors of the jail. You are strip-searched. After that, you are locked down in a cell for 24 hours. During this time, the adrenaline, perhaps the drugs, wear off. All that is left to do is think. Perhaps your family and loved ones are on your mind now – what will happen to them? Maybe there is no one else to think about because all there is in your life is you.

Maybe this describes a similar situation you have been through, or someone that you love has been through. This may be your first encounter with the law, or maybe it is an experience you are all too familiar with. It very well may be that this is the direction your life is headed because you are involved with crime. Whatever your circumstance, Jesus Christ already has you deliverance planned! You are not alone in your struggles and hardships. You have not committed any sin so grievous that the Lord is not willing to forgive. He died for all sins, and freedom is made available to you through Christ.

I have spent a total of twenty-one months in jail when I was in my early twenties. I was involved with crime, drugs, and a host of other sins. Not only did I indulge in these activities as a way of life, but I have dearly loved other people who are involved with these behaviors. I know what it is like to have a mind focused and enthralled by crime, and I know the beautiful contrast of flowing in the mind of Christ. Jesus, Who is Lord of all, set me free from many grievous sins and set my feet upon solid ground. He has given me a purpose higher than anything I could have ever imagined, and I want everyone who reads this book to experience Christ's love for themselves. The life of Christ is a dynamic, life-changing offer, graciously given to you from God Himself.

God has an exciting plan for your life. True Christianity is not boring. On the contrary, it is the most exciting experience I have ever had. I am not speaking of "religion", but of a relationship with Jesus Christ, your Creator. No matter where you are at in your life, Jesus will meet you right where you are. You may be thinking that your circumstances are too dark to invite Him into, but He wants to come into them and transform you.

I pray that you will know the fullness of God's love and his grace. His forgiveness and mercy go beyond words, and His purpose for your life is good. Jeremiah 29:11 states, *"For I know the plans I have for you,' declares the Lord, 'plans to prosper you and not to harm you, plans to give you hope and a future.'"*(NIV)

May God grant you peace, no matter where you are in life – whether it be prison, a psychiatric hospital, a homeless shelter, or your own home.

CHAPTER 1

THE CRIMINAL MIND

All of us were created unique. We all have dreams, hopes and desires. Some of those desires may be for the good, others for not-so-good purposes. However, our behaviors always begin with our thoughts, so that is worth examining.

We all start out the same way as infants. We all have a need for love and affection. We need nurturing and support. Unfortunately, many individuals are deprived of this basic need early on in life. Too many people have miserable beginnings. Perhaps alcohol or drug use was part of how you were raised. Maybe abuse scarred you at an early age until you were old enough to leave that situation. Sadly, many hurting people go on to hurt others. Some go from an abusive home life to another similar situation with their choices in partners. This is not always the case, but often it is.

We were created with emotions, and the need to express those emotions is obvious. Let's say, for example, you grew up in a home where you were told not to cry when you were hurting. Or perhaps you would get screamed at if you spilled a glass of milk. Eventually, under such circumstances, a person learns to suppress their emotions as a protective seal. As they grow older, perhaps they begin to use drugs, alcohol, or sex as a way to cope with their problems. There are many "defenses" that a person can use to numb and avoid the pain of their reality. Such defenses are self-defeating and usually cause more heartache and misery. Still, this is what many individuals do. I was one of them. I coped early in my childhood by indulging in fantasies. In these fantasies, I would create my own reality which was perfect or just how I wanted them to be. Unfortunately, as I grew older, I wanted to live out these fantasies and not cope with reality. Everyday life seemed too boring – I longed for exciting thrills. One of the ways I embraced this life was by lying. And I lied a lot!

Because I was raised in a Christian home and went to a Christian school, I had little experience with crime. When I was twenty-two, I was sentenced to serve two-years-less-a-day. I had never been in jail before and the reality of my situation hit me like a ton of bricks!

I saw many tragic stories of wonderful women suffering from either mental illness, addiction or both. Most of these women had been abused and, it was very common, to hear that they suffered from Borderline Personality Disorder. I would soon discover that I too suffered from this same illness. I was blessed by God to receive treatment from a highly qualified professional, which had many great benefits. I would go as far as to say that this therapy has had a lasting impact on my life.

It was at the correctional facility that I learned a lot of things I had never known before, much of what seemed exciting. Most of these women knew each other and there was the competition of "who-knew-who." I became friends with several of these women and, upon my release, kept in touch with them. We stayed friends after my release and I enjoyed their individual personalities very much. However, I developed a strong addiction to marijuana and experimented with other harsher drugs. I do not blame anyone else for this dilemma, because I am responsible for my own actions. I became fascinated by drug dealers who seemed to have a lot of power. I thought this new life was exciting and met my emotional desire for thrills. I started to play some very dangerous games because I had not been completely set free from my mental illness. I still had to address many issues from my past.

I kept my new life a secret from my psychiatrist for fear that he would judge me. This is not a good example to follow. I eventually lost my parole and had to serve the remainder of my sentence. The sad thing in all of this was that I had an infant child and a fiancé who I could have been a benefit to had I been more stable. But I was captivated by this new way of life. Crime seemed so much more exciting and powerful than everyday life, yet in my heart I knew there had to be more to life than this. I was entertained yet miserable all at the same time.

Then there was God. I was a believer in Christ Jesus and knew that sin was not acceptable, but I felt powerless to change my circumstances. Jesus was my way out of hell, but at the time that was all He was to me. There were moments when I knew His grace and mercy, and at times I would try to read the Bible and devote myself to God. But I enjoyed sin too much, and I liked the feeling of being accepted by people who I felt were "powerful." The ultimate irony of that is the fact that there is nothing or no one more powerful than God Who desired to spend time with me and heal me. He cares about you even if others, or perhaps yourself, do not.

When my husband, Rick, and I were married, I was five months pregnant with my second daughter. I was on probation at the time. I loved him. He was kind and gentle, and he had no serious mental health issues. To me, he was the picture of stability. I began to rely on him for strength instead of God, but it wasn't too long before I became bored with everyday family life. Looking back, I obviously wish I had treated my husband better. By the time our first anniversary came around, I had begun my first of several affairs with a man I felt was more exciting. The affair became known to my husband, and he graciously forgave me and I saw this other man no more.

Because I had tried LSD, I wound up in a psychiatric facility for a while. Shortly thereafter, I was diagnosed with Bipolar Mood Disorder and placed on medication. Over the years, I would frequently go off my meds and get sick again. The drug use added to the problem, and I would find myself in some very dangerous situations. I have been in psychiatric institutions on at least five occasions, so I understand and sympathize with all who suffer from mental illness.

On June 28, 2008, my husband died of a massive heart attack on his way to work. My life seemed shattered. I had no choice but to "shape up" because I was now a single mother. About a year before his death, I had begun an affair with another man, one who I kept on seeing for years. The guilt and shame I felt over this affair cannot be described with words. Suffice to say that I was broken, and Jesus was the One, the only One, who had the power to put all the pieces of my soul back together again.

About a year after Rick's death, I went off my meds again and began to use heavy drugs. I was back in the same routine of lying and living in a fantasy world. My children were removed from my care and placed with my parents. God was keeping my children safe and my family together, but I did not see it that way at the time. To me, I had lost everything. I eventually ended up living in a Second Stage Housing Project, where my mental health deteriorated all the more, despite all the support those around me were trying to offer. I simply would not stop smoking marijuana or take my meds. On December 30, 2010, I decided to end my life. I went into my room and took an entire bottle of mood stabilizers. I woke up in the hospital a day or two later. God had mercy on me and spared my life.

I was admitted into a psychiatric facility where I became stable and started taking my illness more seriously. I began to take my medication and, to this day, have never gone off them. I continued on reading the Bible, and it transformed my life. John chapter one tells us that Jesus is the Word of God, so Jesus Himself healed me. He maintains that health through medication and His Word. It has been almost four years, and I have never been back to a psychiatric facility since. Christ delivered me from drugs, promiscuity and alcohol. I have been reunited with my children and family and am a proud mother of two beautiful daughters who love me dearly. Christ restored my family, healed my mind, and saved my soul. He can do the same for all who call upon His name. Jeremiah 33:3 says, *"Call to me and I will answer you and tell you great and unsearchable things you do not know."* (NIV)

At the beginning of this chapter, I stated that our behaviors begin with our thoughts. Let us now take a look at that. I encourage you to ask yourself, "What am I feeding my mind with? What do I spend my time thinking on?" Our minds are constantly at work, so it is vital that we take an inventory of what we allow ourselves to dwell on. Psalm 119:15 says, *"I meditate on your precepts and consider your ways."* (NIV) How will we know His ways if we do not know His Word? God's thoughts are written down in the Bible, and we know that God is truthful. There is no problem, no struggle, and no temptation that the Bible does not have the answer for. In Matthew 7:7-8, Jesus gives a great promise: *"Ask and it will be given to you; seek and you will find; knock and the door will be opened to you. For everyone who asks receives; he who seeks finds; and to him who knocks, the door will be opened."* (NIV)

If reading the Bible is something new to you, than you are not alone. All students of God's Word had to begin somewhere. I assure you that the journey will be exciting and life-changing. You will begin to experience healing and deliverance. You will understand the meaning of a truly fulfilling life, and you will be astounded at the awesomeness of God! Remember, your thoughts are crucial to your life, so you cannot afford to be passive about this. Romans 12:2 says, *"Do not conform any longer to the pattern of this world, but be transformed by the renewing of your mind."* (NIV) The instructions that God gives us in His Word may seem extremely new to you, but please bear in mind that He is the One Who gave us life and sustains that life.

For some who read this book, a criminal mind is all they have ever known. They may have been raised with it as a way of life and continue on in that mindset. If this describes you, take heart and be encouraged! If you have received Jesus Christ as your Savior, then you have the mind of Christ now. 1 Corinthians 2:16b states, *"But we have the mind of Christ."* (NIV) If you have not yet received Jesus as your Savior, or you are not entirely sure that you have, then I encourage you to go to the last chapter of this book, **Knowing Jesus**, and read that. Then you can come back and pick up in Chapter 2.

The decision of how you want the rest of your life to turn out is up to you. The invitation for Christ to live on the inside of you is open to everyone. You have some choices to make. Choices of how you will think and what you will allow in your life. I'm not saying these choices are easy, but they are worth it. At this point I have to tell you that it is Christ Who will change you. Trust and rely on Him to complete His perfect work in your life. Submit your thoughts to God, and surrender your mind to Him. Trust in Him, He will do it!

Philippians 1:6 "being confident of this, that he who began a good work in you will carry it on to completion until the day of Christ Jesus" (NIV)

NOTES AND REFLECTIONS

NOTES AND REFLECTIONS

CHAPTER 2

ADDICTIONS

*1 Peter 5:8 "Be self-controlled and **alert**. Your enemy the devil prowls around like a roaring lion looking for someone to devour."* (NIV)

There are many kinds of addictions. Addictions to drugs, alcohol, food, sex, pornography, smoking, and a host of many others, often leave people in bondage. For the purpose of this book, we are going to focus on just two – drugs and alcohol.

I am not a qualified addictions councilor. However, I am both a former addict and a student of the Word of God. I have been set free from both drugs and alcohol by Christ Jesus Himself, and He used His Word (the Bible) to do this. I am asking you to look at this from a fresh perspective – God's perspective. His wisdom is supreme, and therefore it is altogether reasonable that we listen to Him concerning these matters. This chapter is dedicated to those beloved souls who are suffering from this crisis. You are very precious to God, and He wants the very best for your life. Suffering from addiction is not in your best interest, nor is it in the best interest of your loved ones.

I am going to show you from Scripture that Jesus sympathizes with your weakness in this area. Hebrews 4:15 says, *"For we do not have a high priest* (Jesus) *who is unable to sympathize with our weaknesses, but we have one who has been tempted in every way, just as we are – yet was without sin."* (NIV) This is a dynamic truth and one we must allow to get deep down into our spirit. He cares! Every time you choose to use drugs or alcohol, He cares.

He is there in your most desperate time of need, even when you miss the mark. The question is, do you care enough about your life to want healing? Christ is more powerful than this addiction, and He has both the strength and the power to set you free.

It is never good to be controlled by something or someone. We have self-control; Self-control is one of the fruit of the Spirit (see Galatians 5:22-23). The Spirit of God lives on the inside of you if you are born again. If your will is there, there is hope. Jesus is alive and well, there is hope! The Apostle Paul says in 1 Corinthians 6:12 *"Everything is permissible for me' – but not everything is beneficial. 'Everything is permissible for me' – **but I will not be mastered by anything.**"* (NIV) If Jesus is your Lord and Savior, then He is now your Master. I will tell you that He is a kind, merciful and loving Master, but He is still Lord of all! We have to learn to come under His authority and respect His commands. His commands are not burdensome; they are worthy of full respect and are always for our benefit, as well as the benefit of others.

You have some choices to make. You most likely will have to avoid some people, places and things for a time, perhaps forever, to stay sober. You will have to form new habits to replace the old behavior patterns that you once engaged in. But, I promise you, it will get easier as time passes. One day at a time is what they teach in recovery groups, and it is actually quite Biblical. Luke 9:23 says, *"Then he said to them all: 'If anyone would come after me, he must deny himself and take up his cross daily and follow me.'"* (NIV) The two key points in this verse are these: **1. You must deny yourself and 2. You must take up your cross daily**

Let me briefly explain what it means to "deny yourself." From God's perspective, you now belong to Him. This should not be a frightening thought. The more you know about Christ and His character, the more you should realize that you are in safe hands! But, we need to recognize the fact that our will is not necessarily God's will. We see the example of obedience that Christ set very shortly before His trial and crucifixion. He was praying in great distress because He knew what was going to happen to Him. In Luke 22:41 we read, *"He withdrew about a stone's throw away from them* (the disciples), *knelt down and prayed, 'Father, if you are willing, take this cup from me; **yet not my will, but yours be done.**' An angel from heaven appeared to him and strengthened him. And being in anguish, he* *prayed more earnestly, and his sweat was like drops of blood falling to the ground. When he rose from prayer and went back to the disciples, he found them asleep, exhausted from sorrow. 'Why are you sleeping?' he asked them. 'Get up and pray so that you will not fall into temptation.'"* (NIV) If I were being tempted to use marijuana again, I would pray the same prayer that He prayed: *Father, not my will, but yours be done!*

Following Jesus is exciting. He will lead you beside peaceful pastures (see Psalm 23) and restore your soul from all the damage sin has caused you. A lot of people are put off by the word "sin." It seems to make them feel guilty. However, as long as you are in this earthly body, you have what the Bible calls a "sin nature" or, in other translations, "the flesh." But sin does not have to have mastery over you, nor do you have to feel guilty or condemned when you fall short. Romans 8:1-2 is beautiful! It says, *"Therefore, there is now no condemnation for those who are in Christ Jesus, because through Christ Jesus the law of the Spirit of life set me free from the law of sin and death."* (NIV)

So, what do we do when we sin? We confess it before God and ask for His forgiveness and it is done! 1 John 1:9 promises this: *"If we confess our sins, he is faithful and just to forgive us our sins and purify us from all unrighteousness."* (NIV) The death of Jesus on the cross was full payment for your sin – you do not have to add to His sacrifice by feelings of guilt and shame. Guilt is unhealthy; conviction, on the other hand, is of the Holy Spirit and leads us to repentance. Repentance means to turn away from something, or to change your mind and attitude about the matter. God's kindness is meant to lead us toward repentance.

"But Melody, this is just so hard – I don't think I can do it!" Luke 18:27 says, *"Jesus replied, 'What is impossible with men is possible with God.'"* (NIV) If you let Christ live through you, the changes that will take place in your life will astound you. Christ in you is the hope of glory! (see Colossians 1:27) It is obvious to anyone that drugs and alcohol are not the solution – they are the problem! For me, it got to the point that I looked for any reason to smoke marijuana. Any reason seemed good enough to me. When there was no stress and I just wanted the pleasant feeling, I would still indulge, telling myself that I deserve a break from life. This went on and on for years until I finally realized that I was sleepwalking through

11

life. I was missing out on all the blessings God had planned for me because I was too "high" to want them.

God wants to use you in His kingdom. You have a place in His heart, and He has a plan for your life. If you are a believer, than there is a harvest of souls out there who need Christ. What are you going to tell them? What are they going to see? For years, people may have seen a phony, hypocritical liar in me. I would try to tell others about Jesus one minute, and then go get "high" with them the next. I was doing more damage to the cause of Christ than I care to think about. Praise God for His mercy and forgiveness!

Ephesians 5:18 says, *"Do not get drunk on wine, which leads to debauchery. Instead, be filled with the Spirit."* (NIV) The Holy Spirit is our Comforter. When we are hurting, He is right there to help us and restore us. Having a clear mind allows the Holy Spirit to speak to us through the Word of God and to our spirits. If we are drunk or "high," we will miss out on what the Lord is trying to tell us. We will miss out on opportunities to serve Him and each other. Proverbs 23:29-35 is a passage any alcoholic can relate to: *"Who has woe? Who has sorrow? Who has strife? Who has complaints? Who has needless bruises? Who has bloodshot eyes? Those who linger over wine, who go to sample bowls of mixed wine. Do not gaze at wine when it is red, when it sparkles in the cup, when it goes down smoothly! In the end it bites like a snake and poisons like a viper. Your eyes will see strange sights and your mind imagine confusing things. You will be like one sleeping on the high seas, lying on top of the rigging. 'They hit me,' you will say, 'but I'm not hurt! They beat me, but I don't feel it! When will I wake up so I can find another drink?'"* (NIV)

There is most likely a root cause as to why you use drugs, alcohol or both. Perhaps it is because of some form of abuse you have suffered, or maybe it is a learned behavior that you saw in your home life early on. It simply is that you are "hooked" on the feeling you get when you use. Whatever the case may be, the time for running is over, if you want it to be. You can be healed emotionally and mentally from any abuse you have suffered through, no matter how tragic or traumatic. If you need therapy and/or treatment, then pursue it. Just please do not leave Christ out of the equation. Allow Him to go to work on your behalf. Place your faith, hope and trust in Him. I guarantee you, He will not disappoint you!

NOTES AND REFLECTIONS

NOTES AND REFLECTIONS

CHAPTER 3

MONEY AND THINGS

Hebrews 13:5 "Keep your lives free from the love of money and be content with what you have, because God has said, 'Never will I leave you; never will I forsake you.'" (NIV)

The Bible has a great deal to say concerning money and possessions. Jesus Himself had much to say about such things when He was on the earth, and His words live on to inspire us and guide us.

Many people are ensnared by their lust for money and material possessions. Their need for things like designer clothes, fast cars, jewelry and whatever else one may accumulate drives them to do many foolish and reckless things. It seems as though these individuals get their value and worth out of the abundance of their possessions. This is not just true of people involved with crime; this is true of many other people out there. When is enough actually going to be enough? What will it take for us to be content?

This chapter of the book is dedicated to all those who are trapped in this vicious cycle. It is with the God-inspired hope that I write to you concerning this matter, and I pray you will open your heart to what the Lord is trying to tell you through His Word. I will prove to you from Scripture that it is possible for you to be content in any and all situations – whether you live in abundance or whether you live in poverty.

In Philippians 4: 11-13, the Apostle Paul makes a wonderful declaration. He states, *"I am not saying this because I am in need, for I have learned to be content in whatever the circumstances. I know what it is to be in need, and I* know what it is to have plenty. **I have learned the secret of being content in any and every situation,** *whether well fed or hungry, whether living in plenty or in want. I can do everything through him who gives me strength."* (NIV)

It is important for you to know that Paul wrote this letter while in prison! (He was put in prison because of his faith in the Lord Jesus Christ.) The entire book of Philippians overflows with joy and enthusiasm. It is four chapters long and I would encourage you to read it. It will strengthen you and give you hope. In the above-noted passage, Paul wrote, *"I have learned the secret of being content in any and every situation."* What is this secret? I believe the contentment Paul is speaking of is the abiding presence of the Lord Jesus through His Holy Spirit Who lives on the inside of every believer. When you are born again and filled with God's Spirit, the Spirit of Jesus, you are never alone – no matter where you are or what circumstances you find yourself in. Jesus is with you no matter what stage of your life you are in! This is vital for you to keep in mind as you continue reading.

Your life in this world, as it exists now, is only temporary. One day, you will leave this world and the Bible tells us that we can certainly take none of our possessions with us. 1 Timothy 6:6-10 says, *"But godliness with contentment is great gain. For we brought nothing into this world, and we can take nothing out of it. But if we have food and clothing, we will be content with that. People who want to get rich fall into temptation and a trap and into many foolish and harmful desires that plunge men into ruin and destruction. For the love of money is a root of all kinds of evil. Some people, eager for money, have wandered from the faith and pierced themselves with many griefs."* (NIV)

You can be materially poor, but spiritually rich! In Revelation 2:9a, Jesus tells the church in Smyrna, *"I know your afflictions and your poverty – yet you are rich!"* (NIV) This is a continuation of the truth He declared when He was on the earth. In Matthew 6:19-21, Jesus says, *"Do not store up for yourselves treasures on earth, where moth and rust destroy, and where thieves break in and steal. But store up for yourselves treasures in heaven, where moth and rust do not destroy, and where thieves do not break in and steal. For where your treasure is, there your heart will be also."* (NIV)

It took me years to grab hold of this truth. The Lord has changed my heart so much on this subject that now my truest treasure in heaven is the Lord Jesus Himself! My heart is with Him and belongs to Him. He is more valuable to me than gold, silver, houses, land, clothes, food, cars and jewelry. His worth goes far beyond words, and His appeal is His love for us. It is the love of God that truly satisfies, and it is a lasting joy and comfort in times of trial, suffering, temptation and need. The love of Christ is the most excellent joy there is!

Let's look at James 4:1-4: *"What causes fights and quarrels among you? Don't they come from your desires that battle within you? You want something but don't get it. You kill and covet, but you cannot have what you want. You quarrel and fight. You do not have, because you do not ask God. When you ask, you do not receive, because you ask with wrong motives, that you may spend what you get on your pleasures. You adulterous people, don't you know that friendship with the world is hatred toward God? Anyone who chooses to be a friend of the world becomes an enemy of God."* (NIV) Wow! What does *friendship with the world* mean? Born Again Christians no longer belong to this world; we belong to the Kingdom of God. The devil, at this time, controls the world and those who do not know Christ as their Savior. The world has its own way of doing things, and God has His way of doing things. Romans 12:2 tell us, *"Do not conform any longer to the pattern of this world, but be transformed by the renewing of your mind."* (NIV) How do we renew our minds from the world we have grown accustomed to and known from infancy? By the Word of God! It is through His Word that you will discover who God is and what His thoughts are. It is through Scripture that we learn new behaviors and learn to think differently. We discover from the Bible who we now are in Christ. In Christ, Who is the Word of God according to John chapter 1, we have a new identity. Embrace this new destiny!

In Luke 12:15 we read, *"Jesus replied, 'Watch out! Be on your guard against all kinds of greed; a man's life does not consist in the abundance of his possessions."* (NIV) We were created to be so much more than the sum of what we own or possess. We all have God-given gifts, talents and abilities. Everyone has something to offer. Perhaps you are in prison at this time. You may be wondering how you can serve Jesus or make a difference in the situation you are in. I assure you, you can! The people you interact with everyday will see the changes Christ is making in you, and they will be drawn to Christ through you. You can share the message of Christ's love (the gospel) right where you are now, both to your fellow inmates as well as to the correctional officers who are in authority over you. God has a marvelous plan for your life – allow Him to work through you!

NOTES AND REFLECTIONS

NOTES AND REFLECTIONS

CHAPTER 4

PROSTITUTION: THE WOUNDED SOUL

1 Corinthians 6:17 "But he who unites himself with the Lord is one with him in spirit." (NIV)

I have never stood on a street corner, but I have engaged in sexual acts in exchange for drugs. This happened to be with only one man, but I can tell you that the effects of these choices caused a great deal of anguish in my soul. I felt completely used and taken advantage of. In addition to that, I felt incredible guilt over my sin. I couldn't believe that I, a professing Christian, could do such things. But I did them just the same. To make matters even worse, this man claimed to be a born again Christian himself. It's conduct like this that causes people who are not saved to mock God. Also, it causes those who are saved to question our salvation. I loved this man, and he claimed to love me, but the true love of Christ does not do things like this to each other. I could have chosen to remove myself from this situation, but I continued on in it for a long time. He did some very kind things for me throughout the years, but this wasn't one of them. He took advantage of my desire for marijuana, and I took advantage of his desire for sex. We used each other.

1 Corinthians 6:18-20 says, *"Flee from sexual immorality. All other sins a man commits are outside his body, but he who sins sexually sins against his own body. Do you not know that your body is a temple of the Holy Spirit, who is in you, whom you have received from God? You are not your own; **you were bought at a price**. Therefore honor God with your body."* (NIV) What

were you bought with? The blood of Christ Jesus! 1 Peter 1:18-19 says, *"For you know that it was not with perishable things such as silver or gold that you were redeemed from the empty way of life handed down to you from your forefathers, but with the precious blood of Christ, a lamb without blemish or defect."* (NIV) So we see from these passages that we belong to God and that our bodies are temples of the Holy Spirit. How should we treat our bodies? God did not intend for our bodies to be violated by others. He wants us to glorify God in our bodies. Romans 12:1 says, *"Therefore, I urge you, brothers, in view of God's mercy, to offer your bodies as **living** sacrifices, holy and pleasing to God – this is your spiritual act of worship."* (NIV)

Sex was created by God to be a beautiful expression of love in marriage. That is what God intends for sex, or love-making, to be. Hebrews 13:4 tells us this: *"Marriage should be honored by all, and the marriage bed kept pure, for God will judge the adulterers and all the sexually immoral."* (NIV) This may be a difficult fact for some to accept, but it is God's Word and, as such, deserves our respect. Is there forgiveness for those who have been sexually immoral? Of course there is! Complete and total forgiveness is for all who have accepted Christ Jesus as Savior and Lord. (See 1 John 1:9) Jeremiah 31:34b is a comforting passage to keep in mind: *"For I will forgive their wickedness and will remember their sins no more."* (NIV)

If you have ever engaged in prostitution or any kind of sexual immorality for that matter, you can be healed from the emotional wounds your soul may have. Jesus can heal you in the deepest regions of your soul and set you free – completely free! If you are not sure you want to be free from prostitution, for whatever the reason, then I implore you to consider your safety.

I am sure you are all too familiar with the chances you are taking with you precious life – a life that God holds very dear to His heart. Perhaps you are a risk taker, or maybe you are so desperate at this time because of addiction, that you are willing to take such gambles with your life. I don't know your circumstances – but Jesus does. He not only is aware of your crisis, but He cares affectionately for you. My heart goes out to anyone, both men and women, who are in the cycle of prostitution. Your Savior has your deliverance already planned and is able to change the desires of your heart. Not only is He able, but He wants to.

This is not intended to cause you any more grief or guilt than you already may be experiencing. Remember Romans 8:1 that assures us that there is no condemnation for those who are in Christ Jesus. My prayer for all who are faced with such issues is that you will come to the realization that you are of great worth in the sight of God. You are so loved by your Heavenly Father that He sacrificed His own Beloved Son to keep you from hell and set you free from this bondage. Whatever stage you are at in this moment of time, please allow Jesus to come in. Let's take a look at a couple of accounts in Scripture where Jesus dealt with women.

Here's a lovely account that reflects Christ's beautiful nature. This is taken from Luke 7:36-50: *"Now one of the Pharisees invited Jesus to have dinner with him, so he went to the Pharisee's house and reclined at the table. When a woman who had lived a sinful life in that town learned that Jesus was eating at the Pharisee's house, she brought an alabaster jar of perfume, and as she stood behind him at his feet weeping, she began to wet his feet with her tears. Then she wiped them with her hair, kissed them and poured perfume on them. When the Pharisee who had invited him saw this, he said to himself, 'If this man were a prophet, he would know who is touching him and what kind of woman she is – that she is a sinner.' Jesus answered him, 'Simon, I have something to tell you.' 'Tell me, teacher,' he said. 'Two men owed money to a certain money lender. One owed him five hundred denarii, and the other fifty. Neither of them had the money to pay him back, so he canceled the debts of both. Now which of them will love him more?' Simon replied, 'I suppose the one who had the bigger debt canceled.' 'You have judged correctly,' Jesus said. Then he turned toward the woman and said to Simon, 'Do you see this woman? I came into your house. You did not give me any water for my feet, but she wet my feet with her tears and wiped them with her hair. You did not give me a kiss, but this woman, from the time I entered, has not stopped kissing my feet. You did not put oil on my head, but she has poured perfume on my feet. Therefore, I tell you, her many sins have been forgiven – for she loved much. But he who has been forgiven little loves little.' Then Jesus said to her, 'Your sins are forgiven.' The other guests began to say among themselves, 'Who is this who even forgives sins?' Jesus said to the woman, 'Your faith has saved you; **go in peace.**'"* (NIV)

When I read that, keeping my own past in mind, I could weep myself! The tenderness of Christ touches me deeply, and I am moved by His compassion and mercy. This is Who your God really is. He is not far off and distant, but lives on the inside of you and loves you just as much as He loves the woman mentioned in the passage above. Let's look at another example of Christ's love and wisdom.

John 8:2-11 says, *"At dawn he appeared again in the temple courts, where all the people gathered around him, and he sat down to teach them. The teachers of the law and the Pharisees brought in a woman caught in adultery. They made her stand before the group and said to Jesus, 'Teacher, this woman was caught in the act of adultery. In the Law Moses commanded us to stone such women. Now what do you say?' They were using this question as a trap, in order to have a basis for accusing him. But Jesus bent down and started writing on the ground with his finger. When they kept on questioning him, he straightened up and said to them, 'If any one of you is without sin, let him be the first to throw a stone at her.' Again he stooped down and wrote on the ground. At this, those who heard began to go away one at a time, the older ones first, until only Jesus was left, with the woman still standing there. Jesus straightened up and asked her, 'Woman, where are they? Has no one condemned you?' 'No one, sir,' she said. 'Then neither do I condemn you,' Jesus declared. 'Go now and leave your life of sin.'* (NIV)

Jesus saved this woman's life! He knew that none of her accusers could honestly say they were without sin themselves, so there was no one who could throw a stone at her. What wisdom and love! This same Jesus offers you forgiveness as well. When you received Christ as your Savior, all your sins were forgiven – past, present and future sins. This is perfect love. May Christ's love set you free and touch you so deeply that you will never be the same!

NOTES AND REFLECTIONS

NOTES AND REFLECTIONS

CHAPTER 5

A PERSON OF TRUTH

Psalm 51:6 "Surely you desire truth in the inner parts; you teach me wisdom in the inmost place." (NIV)

As previously stated, a major problem that once held me in bondage was lying. It was a way of life for me and, for whatever the reason, I practiced this sin since I was a young child. I would exaggerate stories to entertain people; I would tell blatant fabrications to impress those I loved or those whom I wanted to love me. More often than not, these lies presented me in the best light possible. If I wanted sympathy or affection, I would make up stories to people to gratify my desires. I would sometimes present myself as either a victim or an exceptionally desirable individual. Lying is rooted in pride and has no place in the believer's life. Perhaps this is not a struggle for you, but I encourage you to read this chapter anyway. If this is a problem in your life, than please be open to what the Lord wants to show you in His Word.

Lies damage intimacy in relationships. Allow me to explain. One of the people I lied to a lot was my late husband, Rick. In the beginning of our romance, he wasn't altogether interested in a committed relationship. I, on the other hand, wanted a family with this man and had my dreams and hopes fixed on this relationship. So I would lie to him and tell him that other men wanted me, when in fact these were just stories I made up. I tried to make him believe that if he didn't accept me into his life now, someone else would "sweep me off my feet" and he'd lose out. Also, he was separated from his wife at the time and I felt I had to make sure they didn't reconcile, so I would tell outrageous lies about her. While I did eventually get what I wanted because I became pregnant without his knowledge (he thought I was on birth control), I was always left to wonder, "Would he really love me just for me?" He eventually came to know Jesus as His Savior and loved me deeply. It became pretty apparent to him after my arrest that I had a problem with lying and manipulation, so he had a choice to make. He could "throw in the towel" or love me despite my weaknesses. By God's mercy, he chose to love me and became a great support in my life. As my therapy progressed and I learned new ways to cope, I started to develop a more honest relationship with him and our relationship grew stronger. (He was a wonderful daddy and loved his children, as well as me, very much.)

While the particular therapy I was involved with had some very life-changing, positive benefits, it did not directly address the issue of sin. I believe God used this particular therapy to help me dramatically, but there was still the major issue of my life with Christ. I eventually went back to old patterns of behavior, which were very self-defeating and harmful. Drug use did not help; marijuana seemed to open a door into an imaginary world where I could indulge, yet once again, in fantasy and daydreaming. Some of these fantasies seemed relatively harmless. For example, I was not exactly part of the popular crowd in school, so I would fantasize that I was living in a great episode of *Happy Days*, extremely beautiful and married to Fonzie. (Is it any wonder that I wasn't very popular?) Or I would pretend I was married to Lorne Greene from *Bonanza* and lived on the Ponderosa with Pa and the boys. All this was going on during the day when my husband would be at work providing for his family! I needed to get the truth of God's Word deep down into my spirit and have it fill my mind so I could distinguish fantasy from reality and right from wrong. Then I had to choose if I was going to live my life based on the principles of God's Holy Word or not. Praise God that I have determined to live my life in Christ and, as a result, in truth. Christ lives through me, and I am united to Him.

Dishonesty is very harmful to you and others. The Bible has a great deal to say about our words, but let's first look at John 4:23-24: (Jesus speaking) *"Yet a time is coming and has now come when the true worshipers will worship the Father in spirit and in* **truth***, for they are the kind of worshippers the Father seeks. God is spirit, and his worshippers must worship in spirit and in* **truth***."* (NIV) Intimacy with God is the most satisfying life there is and, as previously stated, lying damages intimacy. God knows the truth about every situation before it even happens, so any attempts to lie to God is futile. Practice truth in your relationship with Jesus; this is a good place to start. As you develop the habit of being honest with God about your life and your circumstances in prayer, powerful changes will begin to take place in your life.

Proverbs 6:16-19 says, *"There are six things the Lord hates, seven that are detestable to him: haughty eyes,* **a lying tongue,** *hands that shed innocent blood, a heart that devises wicked schemes, feet that are quick to rush into evil,* **a false witness who pours out lies** *and a man who stirs up dissension among brothers."* (NIV) Please notice that these verses do not say God hates those who practice these things; He hates the sin, not the sinner! Romans 5:8 states, *"But God demonstrates his own love for us in this: While we were still sinners, Christ died for us."* (NIV) Knowing that God's heart is for you and not against you will enable you to trust Him more and more. He's not going to abandon you or leave you (see Hebrews 13:5). Christ Jesus is more committed to His relationship with you than you or I could possibly imagine. Even when we miss the mark and still sin, He gently and tenderly leads us back to Himself. In the Bible, God identifies with himself as the Great Shepherd and we are His sheep. Sheep have a tendency to wonder off, but Jesus makes a great promise concerning this dilemma. In Matthew 18:12-14, Jesus explains it this way: *"What do you think? If a man owns a hundred sheep, and one of them wanders away, will he not leave the ninety-nine on the hills and go to look for the one that wandered off? And if he finds it, I tell you the truth, he is happier about that one sheep than about the ninety-nine that did not wander off. In the same way your Father in heaven is not willing that any of these little ones should be lost."* (NIV)

As with any habit, you have to develop new coping skills to replace the old ones. How should we, as believers, cope with life? In and through Christ Jesus! In John 15:5 Jesus declares, *"I am the vine; you are the branches. If a man remains in me and I in him, he will bear much fruit; apart from me you can do* **nothing.***"* (NIV) If you struggle with wanting to "fit in", take comfort in the fact that you are a part of the family of God. You have a place and God accepts you. You are so precious to Him, and He is the One Who matters. Suppose the truth does not make you very popular for the moment; it is far better to suffer rejection from people than to damage your intimacy with Christ. As a Christian, you can never lose your salvation; you are promised eternal life in John 3:16. Your position as a child of God will **never** change; however, your relationship with the Lord and your fellowship with Him will be affected by sin. Please keep in mind, though, that even with that scenario, Christ has you covered! His forgiveness and mercy go beyond our natural human ability to comprehend. When Jesus was arrested and was on trial for His life, one of His disciples, the Apostle Peter, denied knowing Him three times. He lied the worse kind of lie imaginable. Yet, Christ forgave Him and restored their relationship. You may read about this in John chapter 18. In John 21:15-22, Jesus reinstates Peter as a disciple and appoints him to care for His flock. This is a beautiful example of Christ's unconditional love!

Please understand that this does not mean you have to divulge every aspect of your life to everyone to be a truthful person, nor does it mean you have to divulge other people's confidence either. If people have trusted you with information about their lives, then respect their confidence and do not betray the trust they have shown. Be led by the Spirit of God in this area and use God-given wisdom.

Proverbs 12:19 warns us of the following: *"Truthful lips endure forever, but a lying tongue lasts only a moment."* (NIV) Some natural questions one may ask are these: "Will I ever be trusted again? Can my credibility ever be re-established? Will I ever recover from the shame of being a known liar?" The answer to all these questions is **yes**. With regard to God, He knows if you are telling the truth or not, so you have nothing to fear in that respect. With regard to people, it may take time to re-establish trust in your relationships, but as time passes people will see the remarkable changes that Christ is working in you. Don't give up! Keep moving ahead in Christ and do not fear what people may think. God is your vindicator and will make known your integrity. The freedom of having a clear conscious gives us joy and lasting peace. May you be content in Christ and always abound in hope!

NOTES AND REFLECTIONS

NOTES AND REFLECTIONS

CHAPTER 6

THE PURSUIT OF POWER

Philippians 2:5-11 "Your attitude should be the same as that of Christ Jesus: Who, being in very nature God, did not consider equality with God something to be grasped, but made himself nothing, taking the very nature of a servant, being made in human likeness. And being found in appearance as a man, he humbled himself and became obedient to death – even death on a cross! Therefore God exalted him to the highest place and gave him the name that is above every name, that at the name of Jesus every knee should bow, in heaven and on earth and under the earth, and every tongue will confess that Jesus Christ is Lord, to the glory of God the Father."

As mentioned earlier, one of the elements that drew me into a criminal lifestyle was the pursuit of power. I was tired of being just mediocre and average – I wanted an edge. Seeing as how I was an "unknown" on the street, I aligned myself with individuals whom I felt exuded the kind of power I was seeking. I liked being in an inner circle of "names" who were known out there. I thought that this would give me a sense of belonging, but it was only short-lived. I learned very quickly that some people will just use your innocence as a means of profit.

I learned some very interesting things from these individuals – things that only someone searching to find the meaning amongst the chaos would find. Almost all of the people I was involved with criminally had a strong desire to "look out for number one." The need to be in control was very prevalent. The strong preyed upon the weak. The vulnerable ones were those who had addictions, committing crimes to support their habit. Fear dominated the lives of those souls who owed their drug dealers money. Fear seemed to be the emotional undercurrent of many, except for those who masked their fears so they would not appear weak. To show weakness or vulnerability of any kind made a person a walking target. So to survive, I played off that I was "tough." Nothing could be any further from the truth, but I was good at acting.

You may be wondering, "What was the turning point for you?" The turning point was when I began studying God's Holy Word and understanding the character of Christ. He, who is the ultimate power of the universe, is very kind and tender-hearted. How could I go on living the life I was living and become more like Christ? It can't be done! As I allowed His Spirit to live through me, my heart became soft and pliable in the hands of my Heavenly Father. This is where the rubber meets the road. Living a double life, such as being involved in the criminal world and pursing God at the same time, is futile. A "lukewarm" Christian brings very little glory to the kingdom of God. In fact, such a person can do more damage to the cause of Christ than someone who does not know Jesus at all.

What motivates a person to pursue "power" from criminal activity? I believe that it is rooted in pride. Someone who is what the world would consider to be "average" is the kind of individual who would be drawn to the street. Seeking a name for themselves, they care very little about the consequences that accompany their actions. Lives that are broken and in need of acceptance are the very ones whom Christ desires to bestow His glory upon.

Let's talk about the character of Christ and how His character is developed in us. Let's take a look at Galatians 5:22-23: *"But the fruit of the Spirit is love, joy, peace, patience, kindness, goodness, faithfulness, gentleness and self-control. Against such things there is no law."* (NIV) These qualities define the character of Christ, and a person who is walking in the Spirit will display these attributes in thought, word and deed. I understand these principals do not go hand-in-hand with crime; therefore, a quality decision has to be made. Will you pursue power, or will you pursue Jesus? The choice is yours – a life of misery and heartache, or a life at rest in the heart of God.

Healing is made available through Jesus Christ. No matter what you have done in this life, Jesus wants to forgive and heal you. You do not have to live with feelings of disappointment and sorrow over your past. If you have received Jesus as your Savior, then your past has no power over you. If you feel that you are in a situation that you cannot get yourself out of, that's okay too – Jesus is your deliverer. Whether you are a victim or a perpetrator, you have the opportunity, graciously given to you by God, to begin life anew in Him. He will direct your paths and lead you through your particular set of circumstances. If you have pursued power in all the wrong places, restoration can begin immediately. You may pray the following prayer from your heart:

Heavenly Father,

I have pursued power in very ungodly ways. Please forgive me all my sins. I ask that you would lead me and guide me in my new life – a life that is surrendered to You. Please fill me with Your Holy Spirit and give me a heart of submission to Jesus Christ, who is Lord of all. I pray that you would heal me, as well as heal any individuals that may have suffered because of my actions. Take my life and let it be a testament to Your kindness and goodness. Thank You.

In Jesus' Name,

Amen

NOTES AND REFLECTIONS

NOTES AND REFLECTIONS

CHAPTER 7

A DISCIPLINED SOLDIER

2 Timothy 2:3-5 "Endure hardship with us like a good soldier of Christ Jesus. No one serving as a soldier gets involved in civilian affairs – he wants to please his commanding officer. Similarly, if anyone competes as an athlete, he does not receive the victor's crown unless he competes according to the rules." (NIV)

I struggled most of my life in the area of discipline. Whatever felt good or seemed right to me was what I did, and usually very impulsively. I liked to lie around daydreaming and fantasizing about things that were not healthy or productive. I was lazy and reckless. I had no focus, ambition or determination. I seldom finished what I started, even university. Many excellent opportunities passed me by because I was self-indulgent and unwise with my time. You may not want to hear what I am going to explain to you right now, but it warrants examination. Judge for yourself if what I am telling you is wise or not. The Scriptures I will be quoting basically speak for themselves, and what God says is always wise.

I served my sentence at the Central Nova Scotia Correctional Facility. This particular institution has a military-like set-up. Even the clocks are in military hours. You got up at a certain time, did chores at a certain time, had cell and dayroom inspection, off-duty work activities such as laundry, kitchen, canteen and off-unit cleaning, one hour lock-downs at noon and after supper. This was a radical change of life for me, and I lived this way on both of my stays there (the first being sixteen months and the second five months). It seemed like a total nuisance and I was not enthusiastic about this system at all. Now I realize it has great value if you choose to look at the positive and not the negative.

This system was designed to teach "offenders" discipline and establish a routine. Hebrews 12:11-13 tell us this: *"No discipline seems pleasant at the time, but painful. Later on, however, it produces a harvest of righteousness and* ***peace*** *for those who have been trained by it. Therefore, strengthen your feeble arms and weak knees, 'Make level paths for your feet,' so that the lame may not be disabled, but rather healed."* (NIV) Another passage to keep in mind if you are serving time or will be serving time in such a facility is Ephesians 5:15-17 which says, *"Be very careful, then, how you live – not as unwise but as wise, making the most of every opportunity, because the days are evil. Therefore do not be foolish, but understand what the Lord's will is."* (NIV) A soldier, or any officer for that matter, is a servant. They serve the community and our nation. As Christians, we are now servants (and soldiers) of the Lord Jesus Christ. We are called to serve Him as well as each other. So I propose the following: Let's say, for example, that it is your day to work in the laundry facility. You could take the attitude that this situation is a real pain in the neck, or you could look at it from God's perspective and say to yourself, "I am serving my fellow inmates by washing their clothes." Bear in mind that the Lord Jesus set the example of servant-hood for us by washing His disciple's feet (please read John 13:1-17). Romans 8:28 says, *"And we know that in* ***all*** *things God works for the good of those who love him, who have been called according to his purpose."* (NIV) Your sentence does not have to be a waste of time – it can be a time where you learn new habits and show the love of Christ. (Some of you may look forward to laundry duty and things because it gets you off the unit for a while.) Whatever the case may be, do all things for the glory of God.

Let's look at what it means to submit to authorities. Romans 13:1-5 teaches us the following: *"Everyone must submit himself to the governing authorities, for there is no authority except that which God has established. The authorities that exist have been established by God. Consequently, he who rebels against the authority is rebelling against what God has instituted, and those who do so will bring judgment on themselves. For rulers hold no terror for those who do right, but for those who do wrong. Do you want to be free from fear of the one in authority? Then do what is right and he will commend you. For he is God's servant to do you good. But if you do wrong, be afraid, for he does not bear the sword for nothing. He is God's servant, an agent of wrath to bring punishment on the wrongdoer. Therefore, it is necessary to submit to the authorities, not only because of possible punishment but also because of conscience."* (NIV) A few examples of authority figures would be police, correctional officers, probation officers, parole officers and judges. This may be a drastically new outlook and perspective for you but, trust me, it will go well for you if you practice these things.

There is a spiritual war going on out there for the souls of humankind. How do we fight in this battle? What are our weapons of warfare? Ephesians 6:10-18 explains it this way: *"Finally, be strong in the Lord and in his mighty power. Put on the full armor of God so that you can take your stand against the devil's schemes. For our struggle is not against flesh and blood* (other people), *but against the rulers, against the authorities, against the powers of this dark world and against the spiritual forces of evil in the heavenly realms. (When it says "rulers" and "authorities", it speaks of the devil and his demons.) Therefore put on the full armor of God, so that when the day of evil comes, you may be able to stand your ground, and after you have done everything, to stand. Stand firm then, with the belt of truth buckled around your waist, with the breastplate of righteousness in place, and with your feet fitted with the readiness that comes from the gospel of peace. In addition to all this, take up the shield of faith, with which you can extinguish all the flaming arrows of the evil one. Take the helmet of salvation and the sword of the Spirit, **which is the word of God**. And pray in the Spirit on all occasions with all kinds of prayers and requests. With this in mind, be alert and always keep on praying for all the saints."* (NIV) We see from these Scriptures that God has equipped us spiritually with everything we need to win this battle. In Christ, you have the victory! 1 Timothy 6:12a says, *"Fight the good fight of faith."* (NIV)

God has given you a purpose beyond anything you could have imagined before you knew Christ as your Savior and Lord. Your objective now is to win other souls for Christ and this can only be done through Christ's power. I will close this chapter with Philippians 4:13: *"I can do everything through him who gives me strength."* (NIV)

NOTES AND REFLECTIONS

NOTES AND REFLECTIONS

CHAPTER 8

LOVE

John 15:17 "This is my command: Love each other."(NIV)

There's nothing that I want to know more than what desires are on the Lord's heart. Indeed, there is no other subject more crucial than that of love. But I want to go deeper than the world's idea of love – I want to know love Himself! God doesn't just love, He *is* love. There is no greater expression of His love than that of Christ Jesus. 1 John 2:9-11 declares: *"Anyone who claims to be in the light but hates his brother is still in the darkness. Whoever loves his brother lives in the light, and there is nothing in him to make him stumble. But whoever hates his brother is in the darkness and walks around in the darkness; he does not know where he is going, because the darkness has blinded him."* (NIV) Who wants to go around groping in the darkness? Yet, this is true of many people. Hate is crippling them, but Love can set them free.

There is no hidden agenda with pure love. No selfish motives, no evil intentions and no violence are in the hearts of those filled with Christ's love. His love within us is so supreme that it drives out these feelings and behaviors. In John 13:34-35 Jesus says, *"A new command I give you: Love one another. As I have loved you, so you must love one another. By this all men will know that you are my disciples, if you love one another."* (NIV) Notice that Jesus said in this passage that *"as I have loved you, so you must love one another"*. How in the world can we possibly love the way Jesus loves? I am convinced that this can only be done through His Holy Spirit on the inside of us. It is Christ loving through us. Love is what binds, or unifies, the Body of Christ. Love is more than a pleasant feeling; it is a way of life. But what does this love look like in everyday situations? 1 John 3:16-20 explains it this way: *"This is how we know what love is: Jesus Christ laid down his life for us. And we ought to lay down our lives for our brothers. If anyone has material possessions and sees his brother in need but has no pity on him, how can the love of God be in him? Dear children, let us not love with words or tongue but with actions and in truth. This then is how we know that we belong to the truth, and how we set our hearts at rest in his presence."* (NIV) Action always accompanies love.

You may be telling yourself, *"But if I put myself out there like that, I may get hurt. What if they don't love me back? What if I get hurt or mistreated or taken advantage of?"* (NIV) The truth is that the love of Christ does not fear such things. The true love of Christ within us does not motivate us to be self-centered. You most likely will get hurt at some point. In John 15:12-14 Jesus states plainly, *"My command is this: Love each other **as I have loved you**. Greater love has no one than this, that he lay down his life for his friends. You are my friends if you do what I command."* (NIV) We know that Jesus demonstrated this love for us in His death. He continues this demonstration of love by His life. Such kind of love may seem too radical and extreme to comprehend in the natural mind, but in your heart you know that God's Word does not lie. This kind of love is worth the risk and has many benefits. But, more than that, it is God-honoring and truly satisfying. 1 John 4:18 tells us, *"There is no fear in love. But perfect love drives out fear, because fear has to do with punishment. The one who fears is not made perfect in love."* (NIV) Allowing Christ to love others through us is crucial to being united in Him as the family of God. If you would like to do an in-depth study on love, the entire book of 1 John is highly recommended.

Let us now take a look at the Biblical definition of love. 1 Corinthian 13:4-8b states, *"Love is patient, love is kind. It does not envy, it does not boast, it is not proud. It is not rude, it is not self-seeking, it is not easily angered. It keeps no record of wrongs. Love does not delight in evil but rejoices with the truth. It always protects, always trusts, always hopes, always perseveres. Love never fails."* (NIV) As we can see from this passage of Scripture, love is clearly demonstrated by action. The love of Christ is not passive or self-indulgent; rather, it is eager to express itself in very practical and uplifting ways. Philippians 2:4 tells us this: *"Each of you should look*

NOTES AND REFLECTIONS

NOTES AND REFLECTIONS

CHAPTER 9

UNITY IN THE BODY OF CHRIST

1 Corinthians 12:27 "Now you (plural) *are the body of Christ, and each one of you is a part of it."* (NIV)

It is always nice to be a part of something great! There is no greater cause than that of Christ Jesus, for when it is all said and down, it will come down to this one question: Do you know Jesus as your Savior and Lord? All our struggles, all our burdens and all our pain will be without meaning or purpose if the answer in eternity is "no." If you are searching for a place to fit in, perhaps a family, than I pray this chapter will encourage you.

As believers, God has a unique and marvelous plan for your life and mine, but He also has a plan for us as the Church. These plans should never contradict each other. For example, if you feel that God is calling you to do something, than do it – only do so in His strength and timing. As members of one Body, we all have a role to play in advancing the Gospel of Christ Jesus and making disciples of all people who belong to the family of God. This work is displayed beautifully in the Book of Acts. In all your dreams and endeavors, however, bear in mind what Jesus said in John 15:5: *"I am the vine; you are the branches. If a man remains in me and I in him, he will bear much fruit; apart from me you can do nothing."* (NIV)

In my own personal life, I have come to learn that I am not an island unto myself. My life no longer belongs to me, but to Christ. I am not my own. Thankfully, by the grace and mercy of God, Christ cares for each of us and meets us where we are at. He ministers to us through His

Word and His life, a life that is reflected in and through us by the abiding presence of God's Holy Spirit. Apart from Christ, there is no life. If you are going through a particular time of suffering right now, then please be encouraged by the fact that Christ is with you in this storm, and He will accomplish His perfect plan and purpose in your life and the lives of those whom you love. Let Christ use this time in your life to draw you closer to Himself than ever before and understand that He will use whatever pain you have experienced for His own glory. 1 Peter 5:9-10 says, *"Resist him* (the devil), *standing firm in the faith, because you know that your brothers throughout the world are undergoing the same kind of sufferings. And the God of all grace, who called you to his eternal glory **in Christ**, after you have suffered a little while, will himself restore you and make you strong, firm and steadfast."* (NIV) God will often use your brothers and sisters in the Lord to encourage you; however, do not place your confidence in individuals as your sole means of comfort. Rather, praise God for them but draw your strength and hope from Christ Jesus. Remember that Colossians 1:27 tells us that it is *Christ in you, the hope of glory*! (NIV)

The unity that it is in the Body of Christ is beautiful to behold! For many years, I was drawn to chaos and confusion, leading a very unproductive life and bearing very little fruit. However, as God began showing me the importance of loving our brothers and sisters in the Lord from observing how my church family interacted with each other, I became excited. I wanted into this crowd! I had always had difficulty fitting in with particular groups of people in the past, but in Christ I was loved and accepted not only by Him, but also by His people. This is an awesome testament to God's marvelous order of peace. Allow Christ to bring you to a place of dependence on Him as you go through whatever set of circumstances you find yourself in, with the God-inspired hope and trust that He will turn this around for His glory.

If you are wondering how you "fit in" to God's family, or what role you play in the Kingdom of God, then consider the following passage. 1 Corinthians 12:14-26 tells us this: *"Now the body is not made up of one part but of many. If the foot should say, 'Because I am not a hand, I do not belong to the body,' it would not for that reason cease to be part of the body. And if the ear should say, 'Because I am not an eye, I do not belong to the body,' it would not for that reason cease to be part of the body. If the whole body were an eye, where would the sense of hearing be? If the whole body were an ear, where would the sense of smell be?* **But in fact God has arranged the parts in the body, every one of them, just as he wanted them to be**. *If they were all one part, where would the body be? As it is, there are many parts, but one body. The eye cannot say to the hand, 'I don't need you!' And the head cannot say to the feet, 'I don't need you!' On the contrary, those parts of the body that seem to be weaker are indispensible, and the parts that we think are less honorable we treat with special honor. And the parts that are unpresentable are treated with special modesty, while our presentable parts need no special treatment. But God has combined the members of the body and has given greater honor to the parts that lacked it, so that there should be no division in the body, but that its parts should have equal concern for each other. If one part suffers, every part suffers with it; if one part is honored, every part rejoices with it.*" (NIV)

We see from the passage above that all of us who are believers in Christ Jesus are included in His Body, not excluded. You have a place and you belong. You are accepted and invited into the King's presence, despite your circumstances, because of His shed blood. You are completely justified and cleansed from your sins. God can use you **right where you are** to accomplish His perfect work in your life and in the lives of those around you. Will you let Him?

NOTES AND REFLECTIONS

NOTES AND REFLECTIONS

CHAPTER 10

FREEDOM FROM YOUR PAST

2 Corinthians 5:17 "Therefore, if anyone is in Christ, he is a new creation, the old has gone, the new has come!" (NIV)

I struggled in this area of my life a great deal. I always thought that my past would hinder me from having a productive future. Indeed, at times, I still struggle with guilt, even though I believe that God has forgiven me. I realize the importance of forgiving ourselves and moving ahead. If you feel trapped by your past, then I encourage you to take heart! Jesus has completely forgiven you of any sins you have committed. The world may remind you of your mistakes, your friends and family may remind you, but in Christ, you are totally forgiven and set apart for His good purpose.

The Apostle Paul, before his conversion to Christ, used to violently persecute the Church. He would drag men and women off to prison who believed in Jesus and, when their lives were on the line, he would cast his vote against them. But after he came to know Jesus as his Savior, he wrote the following in Philippians 3:12-16: *"Not that I have already obtained all this, or have already been made perfect, but I press on to take hold of that for which Christ Jesus took hold of me. Brothers, I do not consider myself yet to have taken hold of it. But one thing I do:* **Forgetting what is behind and straining toward what is ahead.** *I press on toward the goal to win the prize for which God has called me heavenward in Christ Jesus. All of us who are mature should take such a view of things. And if on some point you think differently, that too God will make clear to you. Only let us live up to what we have already attained."* (NIV)

If you keep focusing on your past, you will make little progress in the present. Christ has forgiven you. You may still have a punishment handed down to you from the law that you have to carry out, but that does not mean you are any less of a brother or sister in the Lord. You belong to Jesus and His forgiveness is complete. You have a new identity now – you are no longer called to live the way you formerly lived. Does that mean you will always be perfect and never sin again? Of course not! None of us are perfect as long as we live in this body. However, a day is coming when you will meet your Savior face-to-face and you will no longer be reminded of who you used to be. You are free from any guilt or shame associated with your former life. The blood of Jesus Christ has cleansed you from all your sins – past, present and future sins are covered in His blood. There may be consequences if you continue on in rebellion, but you are always going to be God's beloved child. Learn, through God's Word, who you really are in Christ. Your destiny is glorious, if you choose to embrace who you really are and not continue on in the life you once lived. God gave us free-will, and the choice to serve Him wholeheartedly is ours. If you resist His leading, than you will suffer the pain that sin causes an individual. If, on the other hand, you submit to His Divine authority, you will reap a harvest of blessings.

NOTES AND REFLECTIONS

NOTES AND REFLECTIONS

CHAPTER 11

FORGIVENESS

Matthew 6:14-15 "For if you forgive men when they sin against you, your heavenly Father will also forgive you. But if you do not forgive men their sins, your Father will not forgive your sins." (NIV)

To some, this may be the most difficult topic that we have covered thus far. Forgiveness seems unfair to some, because they have been hurt so badly. How could God expect me to forgive so-and-so when he/she has done so much to me? People who are in a state of unforgiveness are actually only hurting themselves. Unforgiveness causes a root of bitterness to spring forth in your soul, and that is more damaging to you than you may realize. It damages your prayer-life and stops you from making significant progress in your walk with God. Jesus warns us of the following in Mark 11:25: *"And when you stand praying, if you hold anything against anyone, forgive him, so that your Father in heaven may forgive you your sins." (NIV)* When we consider all that God has forgiven us for in our lives, and all that he continues to forgive us of, then it should come more easily to us to forgive others.

If the one you are angry with knew how much victory they had over you by your unforgiveness, then they may actually be glad. They are on your mind more than they probably deserve to be anyway, so the wisest thing to do is leave them in the hands of God. If you are deeply wounded by something they have done, Christ is able and willing to heal you of these wounds and set you free. Talk to the Lord about this person. It may not seem fair to you to forgive them, but it is God's way of doing things. James 2:13 says, *"because judgment without mercy will be shown to anyone who has not been merciful. Mercy triumphs over judgment!"* (NIV)

I will suppose, at this time, that you may have some enemies. How should you treat your enemies? Jesus tells us plainly in Matthew 5:43-47: *"You have heard that it was said, 'Love your neighbor and hate your enemy.' But I tell you: Love your enemies and pray for those who persecute you, that you may be sons of your Father in heaven. He causes his sun to rise on the evil and the good, and sends rain on the righteous and the unrighteous. If you love those who love you, what reward will you get? Are not even the tax collectors doing that? And if you greet only your brothers, what are you doing more than others? Do not even pagans do that?"* (NIV) Now that we are in Christ and no longer belong to the world, we must not behave the way the world behaves. This can only be done in the strength of Christ, Who dwells within us. If you struggle in this area, be honest about your situation with the Lord. He will give you new desires and a new attitude. He knows how to keep and guard those that are His!

Let us now take a look at the ultimate example of forgiveness that Jesus demonstrated for us. This is so amazing that it warrants our full attention. This happened when Jesus was being crucified. After He was severely beaten and scourged, they (the Romans) were leading Him away to crucify Him. Crucifixion is an extremely painful death. We read the following in Luke 23:33-34: *"When they came to the place called the Skull, there they crucified him, along with the criminals – one on his right, the other on his left. Jesus said, 'Father, forgive them, for they do not know what they are doing.' And they divided up his clothes by casting lots."* (NIV) Jesus never commands us to do something that He is not prepared to do Himself. He not only tells us to do something; He gives us the strength to do it!

If you would like to settle this matter right now before God, and ensure that your heart is right before the Lord, you may pray the following prayer, or something similar to it:

Heavenly Father,

I forgive all those who have hurt me. I ask you to give me a willing spirit to continue on in an attitude of forgiveness. Please forgive me for all the times I have hurt others. Thank You.

In Jesus' Name,

Amen

NOTES AND REFLECTIONS

NOTES AND REFLECTIONS

CHAPTER 12

SUFFERING

Romans 1:16a "I am not ashamed of the gospel, because it is the power of God for the salvation of everyone who believes" (NIV)

Suffering is something that is unpleasant. It is easy to lose hope during times of suffering, especially when it is prolonged and intense. Many individuals suffer as a result of their own actions, while many are suffering as a result of their faith. There are still others who are suffering because of mental illness or some other kind of sickness or disease. No matter what circumstance you find yourself in, Jesus can take your pain and turn it into victory! God can use any set of circumstances for a purpose higher than what we could ever expect. It is comforting to know that all the pain we experience in life does not have to be pointless. When it has all been said and done, how we have endured these times of suffering will be the question that others will ask of us.

The Bible has a great deal to say about suffering. Let us take a look at several passages that help to shed light on this subject. 1 Peter 4:14-16 says, *"If you are insulted because of the name of Christ, you are blessed, for the Spirit of glory rests on you. If you suffer, it should not be as a murderer or thief or any other kind of criminal, or even as a meddler. However, if you suffer as a Christian, do not be ashamed, but praise God that you bear that name."* (NIV) I know what it is like to suffer as a criminal, as a result of my own choices. Yet, all the time I suffered, Christ did not leave me or abandon me through any of it. He used my time in jail to teach me many things about Himself that I had not known before. However, I was captivated by the new way of life that I saw, so I made more choices that were unhealthy after I was released. You see, God has very graciously given us a free-will; we can choose to obey him as so be blessed, or we can choose to resist His leading and ignore His authority and suffer the consequences. One thing was for sure – I was determined to never go back to jail again! Now that I am in a healthier place in my life, my heart is with those who are still suffering as a result of their crime(s). It is my heart's desire to minister to all those beloved souls who are in anguish in jail or in prison, and I desire to bring them a message of hope.

Now that you have received Christ as your Savior and want to live for Him, you may experience a new kind of suffering, one that brings joy to the heart! 1Peter 2:19-23 tells us this: *"For it is commendable if a man bears up under the pain of unjust suffering because he is conscious of God. But how is it to your credit if you receive a beating for doing wrong and endure it? But if you suffer for doing good and you endure it, this is commendable before God. To this you were called, because Christ suffered for you, leaving you an example, that you should follow in his steps. 'He committed no sin, and no deceit was found in his mouth.' When they hurled their insults at him, **he did not retaliate; when he suffered, he made no threats. Instead, he entrusted himself to him who judges justly**."* (NIV) If crime is a way of life for you, you suffer every day. You may not realize all the pain you are enduring at that particular moment in time, but when the jail door slams shut behind you, you realize very quickly the consequences of your actions. If you are willing to take risks with your life for such purposes, why not shift your focus onto Him Who is able to save you and your loved ones?

Because I lived impulsively for so many years, I know what it is like to get caught up in the moment and be reckless. Proverbs 14:15 says, *"A simple man believes anything, but a prudent man gives thought to his steps."* (NIV) I have lived in a very "simple" way, but now Christ has taught me through this verse that it is wise to think about our impulses before we act on them. Our decisions not only impact our own lives, but they seriously play a role in the lives of those we love and care about. I have learned that there is a greater good out there, higher than that of my own selfish existence. While it is important to care for myself, it is also important to care for others. Philippians 2:4 says, *"Each of you should look not only to your own interests, but also to the interests of others."* (NIV) This is a way of life for those who live for Christ; His love in our hearts compels us to care for each other.

Christ Jesus is the ultimate example of what it means to display love by our actions. You may suffer rejection, insult and mockery when others find out that you have surrendered your life to Christ, but this kind of suffering produces in us a depth of character that we need to recognize. Romans 5:3-5 is very promising: *"Not only so, but we also rejoice in our sufferings, because we know that suffering produces perseverance; perseverance, character; and character, hope. And hope does not disappoint us, because God has poured out his love into our hearts by the Holy Spirit, whom he has given us."* (NIV)

If you are undergoing a time of suffering right now, than I encourage you to allow Christ to come into your particular set of circumstances, no matter what they are. He will meet you exactly where you are at; but, He also loves you too much to allow you to remain there. He will lead you along the paths of righteousness for His name's sake (see Psalm 23), and He will live through you. By His divine strength, you will make it through whatever storm you are presently facing. Jesus is the Prince of Peace!

NOTES AND REFLECTIONS

NOTES AND REFLECTIONS

CHAPTER 13

CHRIST IS BEAUTIFUL IN YOU

Psalm 45:2a "Thou art fairer than the children of men" (KJV)

The world has a different standard for beauty than what Christ does. To Jesus, you are beautiful because He created you. Psalm 139:13-16 says, *"For you created my inmost being; you knit me together in my mother's womb. I praise you for I am fearfully and wonderfully made; your works are wonderful, I know that full well. My frame was not hidden from you when I was made in the secret place. When I was woven together in the depths of the earth, your eyes saw my unformed body. All the days ordained for me were written in your book before one of them came to be."* (NIV) God planned your existence before the world was ever created – you are not a mistake! He loves you with an unfailing love, and He desires that you find your value and worth in Him.

I struggled for many years with a very poor self-image. I did not like certain things about my looks, and I felt inferior to other women that I thought were more beautiful than me. Now, however, the more I begin to see myself through the Lord's eyes and realize that He is the One whose opinion matters most to me, than I start to relax and feel more comfortable in my own skin. Keeping up with what the world considers to be beautiful is exhausting and futile. There is a beauty that goes beyond the exterior – the beauty of inward adornment, the heart of a person.

I have never seen Jesus, but in my heart I know that He is beautiful. His character and all that He stands for are absolutely breath-taking and inspiring. My aim is to be like my Creator in thought, word and deed – keeping in mind that it is His Spirit Who beautifies my inner person. The more time that I spend with Jesus in prayer and in His Word, the more beautiful I feel. His acceptance and unconditional love give me the strength I need to go out into the world and not fear rejection from others. I do not want to draw people to "Melody" but to Jesus – the One Who is willing to save them.

In Psalm 27:4, the psalmist declares his heart's desire this way: *"One thing I ask of the Lord, this is what I seek: that I may dwell in the house of the Lord all the days of my life, **to gaze upon the beauty of the Lord** and to seek him in his temple."* (NIV) As previously mentioned in chapter 4, our bodies are temples of the Spirit of God. This is a marvelous truth – that Christ's Spirit is with us no matter where we are or what we are doing. Jesus never violates our will, and His presence is so gentle that we often do not realize He is there – but He is! He loves you even during those times that you do not love yourself, and it is His love that sustains and upholds you.

Please do not misunderstand me. I do not think that there is anything wrong in looking your best. I wear make-up and fix my hair and such, but that is not where my beauty comes from. I do not depend on those things for my value and worth. I depend on Christ in me to be my confidence. Any gifts, talents or abilities I have are all given to me from God, so I depend on Him to maintain what He desires for me to achieve. It is faith in His strength that I put my trust, not in myself. Philippians 3:3 says, *"For it is we who are the circumcision, we who worship by the Spirit of God, who glory in Christ Jesus, and who put no confidence in the flesh"* (NIV) If I were to put confidence in my own strength and capability, I would be on very shaky ground because I know all too well my own weaknesses. But I do not fear failure, because my relationship with Jesus is not based on my performance, but on His strength to handle whatever set of circumstances I find myself having to face. If I fall down, He is there to pick me up. When I resist and rebel against His will and fall flat on my face, He reaches down and lifts me back up again. He does not reject me, even when I am disobedient to His Divine authority. Reflecting upon the subject of obedience, however, I have become convinced that it is Christ Who gives me the desire to live an obedient life. This desire springs forth from the love and respect that I have for Him, because I am learning more and more just Who it is who has saved me!

Another trap that I used to fall into was comparing myself to others. I would try to compete and, if I felt like I did not meet my desired goal, than I would be very discouraged. Having an over-estimated opinion of myself and my talents was just as damaging as having a poor self-image. By God's grace, I have learned to be myself and not to try to be someone else – which was what I had done the majority of my life. I am at peace with myself now because I have come to understand that God wants me to be the person that He created me to be. His plan for my life leaves no room for me to live in a dream-world where I control everything, including how I look. We were all created unique, and it is variety that is the spice of life.

Jesus is altogether lovely and worthy of praise. His personality and nature reflect all that I would desire to be like. His example of how to live in this world raises the standard of what we ought to become. All that is beautiful is a reflection of His glory, and it is in Him that I put my confidence. My prayer for you is that you will understand just how beautiful you really are in the sight of God, and that His life within you will bring honor to His Name. May you find peace in knowing that Christ has accepted you, just the way you are, and He will make you whole and complete in Him. Christ is beautiful in you!

NOTES AND REFLECTIONS

NOTES AND REFLECTIONS

Chapter 14

Jesus is Coming Back

John 14:2-3 "In my Father's house are many rooms; if it were not so, I would have told you. I am going there to prepare a place for you. And if I go and prepare a place for you, I will come back and take you to be with me that you also may be where I am." (NIV)

The subject of the Lord's return is something that has caused much controversy over the years. It seems so hard for people to accept that Jesus will physically reign forever on this earth one day, as King of kings and Lord of lords. It seems that we are so caught up with the cares of this life that we seldom give thought to our eternal future – a future that has great hope and promise for those who have accepted Jesus as their Savior. The promise of the Lord's return is throughout the entire Bible, and in light of the days we are living in, deserves our attention.

I do not claim to be an expert in Bible prophecy, but I have studied the Word of God on this subject, as well as listened to many great teachers concerning this topic. I will share with you some of what I know, but I encourage you to study further in this area yourself. It is worth the investment of your time, and I pray you will be encouraged with what you discover.

The Lord has promised us in His Word that one day He will come in the clouds and gather together with Him all those who have believed in Him. This event is known as the Rapture and is found in 1 Thessalonians 4:16-18: *"For the Lord Himself will come down from heaven, with a loud command, with the voice of the archangel and with the trumpet call of God, and the dead in Christ will rise first. After that, we who are still alive and are left will be caught up together with them in the clouds to meet the Lord in the air. And so we will be with the Lord forever. Therefore encourage each other with these words."* (NIV) Let us examine this verse in detail. We see from this passage that it is Jesus Who will gather us to be with Him. When it says that the "dead in Christ will rise first," we may reasonably ask the question: Where are those who have died believing in Christ? Their spirit is with Jesus in heaven, but the earthly tent they had lived in (their body) is in the ground. Thus, the Resurrection Power of Christ Jesus is seen at work in the event of the Rapture. Their bodies will be raised to life, never to perish again. Philippians 3:20-21 says, *"But our citizenship is in heaven. And we eagerly await a Savior from there, the Lord Jesus Christ, who, by the power that enables him to bring everything under his control, will transform our lowly bodies so that they will be like his glorious body."* (NIV) Immediately after the dead are raised first, then we who have put our faith in Jesus and are still alive will be changed. The Apostle Paul describes this change in 1 Corinthians 15:51-52: *"Listen, I tell you a mystery: We will not all sleep* (die), *but we will all be changed – in a flash, in the twinkling of an eye, at the last trumpet. For the trumpet will sound, the dead will be raised imperishable, and we will be changed."* (NIV)

The question that may arise is this: What happens to those who have not accepted Jesus as their Savior? The Bible tells us that there will be a 7-year Tribulation period for earth dwellers. During this time, God will pour out His wrath on a world that has rejected Christ. We see in the book of Revelation that it is possible to receive Jesus as your Savior during this time, but it will still be a time of horror. The vast majority of people who receive Jesus as their Savior during this time will die for their faith. The Anti-Christ, who will be a global dictator during this time, will cause all people to receive his mark on their right hand or on their foreheads. This is known as the mark of the Beast and is described in Revelation 13:16-18 *"He also forced everyone, small and great, rich and poor, free and slave, to receive a mark on his right hand or on his forehead, so that no one could buy or sell unless he had the mark, which is the name of the beast or the number of his name. This calls for wisdom. If anyone has insight, let him calculate the number of the beast, for it is man's number. His number is 666."* (NIV) (The reason that John, the writer of Revelation, uses the word "forced" instead of "will force," is because he is describing what he saw in a vision from

Jesus.) Once a person receives this mark during the tribulation, he sells his soul to the devil and salvation is no longer possible. The consequence for receiving this mark is in Revelation 14:11: *"And the smoke of their torment rises for ever and ever. There is no rest day or night for those who worship the beast and his image, or for anyone who receives the mark of his name."* (NIV) John then goes on to say in verse 12 of chapter 11 this: *"This calls for patient endurance on the part of the saints who obey God's commandments and remain faithful to Jesus."* (NIV) So the time to accept Christ as your Savior is now, not during this terrible time in history.

At the conclusion of the 7 year Tribulation, Christ Jesus will return with the Church and establish His Kingdom. You may read about this glorious event in Revelation chapter 19. If you want to be on the winning side of this scenario than you should, without a doubt, consider carefully your decision on receiving Jesus as your Savior. Your eternal future hangs in the balance of this one decision.

I have been mocked for telling others about the return of Christ, but it makes no difference to me. I will continue to tell others of this important truth because they have a right to know what the Lord has planned. Most scholars of Bible prophecy believe that we are currently living in the last days before Christ's return. This should prompt us to tell others about the saving power of Jesus Christ before it is too late. Those that would call me crazy are proving my point and confirming that we are indeed living in the End Times. 2 Peter 3:3-4 states, *"First of all, you must understand that in the last days scoffers will come, scoffing and following their own evil desires. They will say, 'Where is this "coming" he promised? Ever since our fathers died, everything goes on as it has since the beginning of creation.'"* (NIV) I believe God's Word, and I know that what He has told us will take place, whether or not others choose to accept it. I encourage you to search this matter out for yourself to see if these things are so. There are many excellent resources out there to assist you, the most important being the Bible. Let me close this chapter with the following passage, one that I hope will encourage you: *2 Timothy 4:7-8 "I have fought the good fight, I have finished the race, I have kept the faith. Now there is in store for me the crown of righteousness, which the Lord, the righteous Judge, will award to me on that day – and not only to me, but also to all who have longed for his appearing."* (NIV)

NOTES AND REFLECTIONS

NOTES AND REFLECTIONS

CHAPTER 15

KNOWING JESUS

John 3:16-17 "For God so loved the world that he gave his one and only Son, that whoever believes in him shall not perish but have eternal life. For God did not send his Son into the world to condemn the world, but to save the world through him." (NIV)

We all were created to live forever. Where you choose to spend eternity is up to you. God has made a way for us to receive Salvation, and that way is summed up in just one word – Jesus! John 14:6 says, *"Jesus answered, 'I am the way and the truth and the life. No one comes to the Father except through me."* (NIV) Here we see that there are not many ways to heaven, just one way – through Jesus!

Romans 3:22-25a tells us this: *"for all have sinned and fall short of the glory of God, and are justified **freely** by his grace through the redemption that came by Christ Jesus. God presented him as a sacrifice of atonement, through faith in his blood."* (NIV) If we are honest with ourselves, we know that we have all sinned. As such, because of God's holiness, we deserve death and eternal separation from God. But God loved us so much that He sent His Son, Jesus (Who is God in the flesh), to die for our sins. He took our punishment upon Himself and this sacrifice was acceptable to the Father because Jesus had never sinned! This is the ultimate demonstration of love. God raised Him to life on the third day and now, if we simply receive Christ into our hearts, we will be forgiven of all our sins – past, present and future. The offer is open to everyone who believes in Jesus. Instead of going to hell, we can spend eternity with Jesus Christ. Let me use a story to help you understand this.

Suppose you had killed someone. You are guilty and the Judge is about to sentence you to death. You are there in the courtroom at your sentencing, knowing full well that you deserve this punishment. It is justifiable, according to the law. (I know that there is no death penalty in Canada but, for the purpose of this analogy, please humor me.) Now, before you are taken away to prison to be executed, someone who you do not know comes forward and pleads your case before the Judge. He says to him, "I will go in his/her place. I will carry out their sentence for him/her. I will die for this person. Allow him/her to go free." This person is unknown to you, be he knows who you are and loves you. Keep in mind that this person is completely innocent and has never committed a single crime in his life. Amazingly, the Judge accepts the offer and you are given the offer to go free. Not only can you go free, but you will have no criminal record! This is what it means to be justified by grace. This is what Jesus has done for you. But, you have to accept this offer. You could reject it and die (there is no parole in hell by the way), or you can simply accept this gracious act of mercy. What seems more reasonable to you?

If you accept Christ, His Spirit comes to live on the inside of you, guaranteeing that you will never be separated from God. Colossians 1:27 says, *"To them God has made chosen to make known among the Gentiles the glorious riches of this mystery, **which is Christ in you, the hope of glory**."* (NIV) The Holy Spirit lives on the inside of every believer.

If you want to receive Jesus as your Savior and Lord, you can pray the following prayer from your heart:

Lord Jesus,

I admit that I am a sinner. I believe that you died for my sins and were raised to life on the third day. Please forgive me all my sins. Come into my heart and be my personal Lord and Savior. Thank you, my Lord.

In Your Name I pray,

Amen

If you prayed that prayer, than welcome to the family of God! You are now a son or daughter of the Most High God, and you belong to Christ. Nothing will ever separate you from His love. You may not "feel" anymore different now than before you prayed it, but there has been a tremendous difference that has taken place. You were once dead in your trespasses and sins, but now God has made you alive in Christ. This is a matter of faith. God bless you.

Romans 8:38-39 "For I am convinced that neither death nor life, neither angels nor demons, neither the present nor the future, nor any powers, neither height nor depth, nor anything else in all creation, will be able to separate us from the love of God that is in Christ Jesus our Lord." (NIV)

NOTES AND REFLECTIONS

NOTES AND REFLECTIONS

NOTES AND REFLECTIONS

CONCLUSION

I want to leave you with one final plea – one that is of benefit to you.

There are two roads ahead of you. One road leads to despair, and the other road leads to eternal life. You could keep on doing the same things that you have always done, things of the sinful nature. That choice is up to you. You have a free will. Drugs, pre-marital sex, greed and many other things that the devil wants you to indulge in are yours for the taking. But the question I ask you is this: What is the end result of those things? I can promise you that whatever fleeting pleasure you receive from these "enjoyments" will ultimately end in misery. The world does not have your best interest at heart, but Jesus does. His love will enable you to over-come the temptations of the flesh and enter into peace. And what a gift His love is to us! He loves you with a love so divine that no human author could communicate it to you in all its fullness.

Your other option is eternal life. This guarantees you that you will not go to hell when you die, or be left behind here on earth when the rapture takes place. But eternal life is more than that – it can be enjoyed now. It is the life of Christ in us that overcomes our weaknesses and gives us strength for our daily living. How sweet eternal life is!

For most of you who read this book, I will not have the privilege of meeting you and giving you a hug or a spoken word of encouragement. But if I could look you in the eye and you could see the sincerity of my heart, as it concerns your welfare, than you would see the evidence of what Christ is capable of doing. I am not an overly-talented individual, nor am I more valuable than you in the sight of God. I am simply, and wonderfully, a born again, Holy Spirit-filled follower of Christ Jesus who loves to share

God's love with people. I have seen what state the world has left me in when I chose the things that it promotes. But, even greater than that, is the state that I am in now – peaceful, in love with Jesus and mentally sound. Christ, the healer, has performed miraculous things on my behalf, and He is willing and able to do the same for you. This is your life, and you only get one. I pray that your life will be turned over to the Lord, and that you will experience joy in all its fullness.

Amazing Grace
How sweet the sound
That saved a wretch like me!
I once was lost
But now am found
Was blind but now I see.

- John Newton

A MESSAGE FROM PASTOR IAN MACFARLANE

__Who Am I really__

Who are You?
Really! Who are You?
It seems like an obvious question, almost idiotic to ask!
If we were asked that question, we'd point to ourselves and say this is who I am. But is that really you?

Our world has a tendency towards being very superficial, never really getting to know each other, just knowing one another on the surface. Like looking at the perfect birthday cake and never taking a bite

When you really think about who you are,...it doesn't come from the outside it comes from the inside. Your body is simply an expression of who you are and what you believe from the inside.

Melody asked me to explain the abiding life, which is also known as the dependent life, the life of rest, the life of Christ, or the Spirit-filled life. All these terms describe something that many people have never experienced.

But to understand this you have to begin with who you were created to be and you weren't created to be(which is who you are now).

You were created with much more than what you're experiencing now

In Colossians 1:26-27 the apostle Paul talks about the "mystery" of God that has been kept hidden for ages but is now revealed.

Paul says God has chosen to make known to us.. "the glorious riches of this mystery, which is Christ in you, the hope of glory."

What does that mean? Christ in You the hope of glory!

That can seem like as much of a mystery as the mystery itself...but it really is quite simple, glory refers to the character of God, Hebrews 1:3 says *"The Son radiates God's own glory and expresses the very character of God, and he sustains everything by the mighty power of his command. When he had cleansed us from our sins, he sat down in the place of honor at the right hand of the majestic God in heaven."* NLT

So what "Christ in you the hope of glory" simply means is Christ in you the hope of God's character in you.

You were originally created to express the image and the character of God. Genesis says that God made you in His image. God is Spirit. So if we were created in God's image, we were created with His Spirit living though us in perfect union with God

Charles Price uses a great illustration about this, Adam an Eve were created in the image of God.

God is spirit so if they were created in His image what does that mean? It means they were created with His character

Now suppose you and I had a time machine and could go back in time to where it all started, the Garden of Eden, before the fall of man before sin came into the world. Suppose we got out of the time machine, then hid behind a bush and watched the way Adam and Eve acted and interacted with one another, the way they treated each other.

If we could do that we would see what God was like because they were created in His image. They showed His character. They acted and treated one another the way God would.

The sin and selfishness, self awareness that came from the fall took away all that...we ceased to express the selfless image of God and now express the selfish self-centered image of ourselves. All we have to do is look around to see how destructive and damaging we are because of selfishness

When Christ died on the cross he said "it is finished!" the work is done, the debt to God for our sin had been paid, and we are made right, we are justified with God. And because we are justified, God can complete His restoration project in our lives.

Through Christ's death and resurrection paying the penalty for our sin and giving us the righteousness of Christ, Jesus can now give us His indwelling Spirit, His glory, His image, His character.

Christ gives us His Spirit to think for us, to live for us in this messy world, to order our days and enjoy His life the way we were meant to.

It means that in the midst of terrible circumstances I can have absolute peace, because Christ's Spirit indwells me and lives for me.

2Peter1:3 *His divine power has given us everything we need for a godly life through our knowledge of him who called us by his own glory and goodness.*NIV

Jesus said *"Come to me, all you who are weary and burdened, and I will give you rest. Take my yoke upon you and learn from me, for I am gentle and humble in heart, and you will find rest for your souls."* Matthew 11:28-29 NIV

When we come to end of our own striving and struggling and in exhaustion give up on trying to make this life work, and simply trust and depend on Him, His life lives through us, for us and as us and real life happens, abundant life, a life of joy and contentment and satisfaction.

The writer Watchman Nee had a great illustration for the abiding life, what it means to have the life of Christ living in and through us

Roman 8:1-2 says *Therefore there is now no condemnation for those who are in Christ Jesus. ² For the law of the Spirit of life in Christ Jesus has set you free from the law of sin and of death.*NIV

The life of Christ in you is a law; sin is a law...what makes something a law

It's a law when it happens 100% of the time

Gravity is a law...Anywhere you go in the world you will feel the effects of gravity. It wants to hold you here on the earth you're not going up in the sky

But planes fly – how is that possible? Gravity is saying no you are not going up in the air

Planes fly because there is another law at work the law of aerodynamics— that with enough propulsion and the correct lift design on the wings of a plane,... planes can fly!

Think of sin as the law of gravity and Jesus as the plane with infinite propulsion

As we depend on Christ and His life lives through us, we have victory over sin, The life of Christ is a law that over comes the law of sin and death – it is only as we abide in Christ that this happens when we try and live out of our own strength we wither, only Christ's life is victorious

So the message for us is to stop trying and start trusting

Galatians 2:20 says "*I have been crucified with Christ and I no longer live, but Christ lives in me. The life I now live in the body, I live by faith in the Son of God, who loved me and gave himself for me.*"NIV

The moment I believe in Christ to save me I am crucified with Christ on the cross, my old man - my sinful selfish nature is dead, it has no more controlling power over me and I live by the faith the God gives me, trusting, depending, abiding(remaining) in Him. But there is even more here in the verse. It says He loved me and gave himself for me. We typically understand "gave" to mean that He gave Himself for me when He died on the cross for my sin. The Greek word for gave here is in the second aorist tense, active voice. That means that the "giving" is continuous. He "gave", He "gives" and He will give himself for me.

His indwelling Spirit will live for me and through me. He is responsible for me. He is responsible for you if you simply stop striving in your own effort and let Him be enough for you.

What Christ wants you to hear today more that anything else is that He is enough – Jesus is enough! The question is will we let Him? Will You?

ABOUT THE AUTHOR

Melody Wolfe is a Christian author who is very passionate about the direction the Lord is taking her. She is blessed to have a wonderful family who support her and love her. She is a proud mother of two daughters.

Melody is a member of Living Hope Community Church and is actively involved in ministry. The Lord has given her a great desire to support her community, and she is dedicated to proclaiming the Gospel of Jesus Christ to any who are willing to listen. She is an active student of the Word of God and has a heart for those living with mental illness and addiction. Her prayer is that the Lord will reach those individuals who are actively involved in crime with His love, mercy and forgiveness.

You may learn more about Living Hope by visiting their website at: www. livinghopehalifax.com

Feel free to contact Melody at: melodywolfe@outlook.com

Notes and Reflections